DAY TRIPS TO HEAVEN

*To Celia
With love
from
Grandma Rita*

Day Trips to Heaven

FIRST CLASS · DAY RETURN

Celebrity Dreams of Getting Away From It All

MarshallPickering
An Imprint of HarperCollinsPublishers

First published in Great Britain in 1991 by Marshall Pickering

Marshall Pickering is an imprint of
HarperCollinsReligious
part of HarperCollins*Publishers*
77-85 Fulham Palace Road, London W6 8JB

Copyright in the compilation © 1991 HarperCollins*Publishers*

The Authors assert the moral right to be identified as
the authors of this work

Printed and bound in Great Britain by
HarperCollins Manufacturing, Glasgow

A catalogue record for this book is available from the British Library

CONDITIONS OF SALE

This book is sold subject to the condition that it shall not, by way of trade
or otherwise, be lent, re-sold, hired out or otherwise circulated without
the publisher's prior consent in any form of binding or cover other than
that in which it is published and without a similar condition including
this condition being imposed on a subsequent purchaser.

VICTORIA WOOD

Comedienne

Dreams of going straight in . . .
"I've no idea, but I don't mind what it's like as long as you don't have to queue for a ticket."

V Wood

MILES KINGTON
Journalist

Miles Kington's dreaming of a white heaven. He imagines...
"turning up at my local station, Bath Spa, to get the London train and hearing an announcement: 'We regret that all diesel and electric locomotives have been temporarily withdrawn from service and we are forced to supply a steam hauled service today,' then seeing a long Pullman train draw in hauled by two venerable GWR engines, getting into a comfortable old leather-and-wood compartment and setting off, when suddenly the door opens and the guard says: 'Mr Kington?' Upon my saying yes, he gives me a large parcel with my name on, tips his hat and goes off. Inside the parcel, as if by magic, I find all the things I have lost and broken in my life – treasured jazz records, valued letters, favourite old mugs, vanished photographs – and when the guard returns, I say to him: 'Who are you?' He winks and starts taking off his uniform to reveal that underneath he has a red robe, a white beard and bells. 'So there really is a Father Christmas?' I gasp. 'Of course', he says and points out of the window, where I see to my surprise that it is snowing thickly. We stop at a snowy station and there waiting for me are my father and mother, which is something of a surprise as they were divorced and died some time ago, but here they are again, much younger than me now and good friends again.

On seeing me they say in unison: 'Have you written your thank you letter to Aunt Mary yet for the watch she gave you in 1962?' and I am just about to say no, rather shamefully, when my eye falls on the big box the guard gave me, in which I see not only the watch (which I lost in 1970) but the thank you letter I never wrote, and I give it to them through the window. My father is halfway through reading it when a large reindeer leans over his shoulder and eats it. 'He loves thank you letters,' says Father Christmas, clipping everyone's tickets. 'You can imagine, there isn't much else to eat at the North Pole. Change at Didcot, for Didcot.' I am just trying to puzzle this one out when a man in a white coat appears and says 'Take your seats for the first sitting of Christmas lunch please – the restaurant is two carriages down.' Moments later I am being served a glass of champagne and pulling the most enormous cracker in the world, out of which steps my wife, saying 'I'd better go and see if the turkey is overcooked,' but I say (CONTINUED NEXT VOLUME. . .)
"

MURRAY ARBEID

Fashion Designer

Murray Arbeid's heaven is ...
"to be somewhere where no one is remotely interested in fashion, clothes, food, chic, smart etc, etc, etc, – Bliss!"

SUE TOWNSEND

Writer

Adrian Mole's creator has a secret dream of...

"a communist world which recognised individuality – how's that for an impossible dream? Heaven would be every world citizen having food, water, main drainage and somewhere to live. My personal heaven would have books and Black Magic chocolates (I'm a diabetic so chocolates are forbidden). And young people to talk and laugh with. I hope heaven has a 'smoking area' because if I'm already dead I can smoke to my heart's content. I hope Dostoevsky and Chekhov are in heaven."

G. M. GILL

Chief Cashier, the Bank of England

All aboard for glory...
THE SPIRITUAL RAILWAY
(From a tablet in Ely Cathedral, 1845)

"The line to heaven by Christ was made,
With heavenly truth the Rails are laid,
From Earth to Heaven the line extends
To Life Eternal where it ends.

Repentance is the station then
Where Passengers are taken in,
No fee for them is there to pay
For Jesus is Himself the Way.

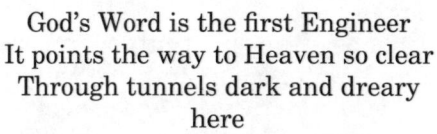

God's Word is the first Engineer
It points the way to Heaven so clear
Through tunnels dark and dreary here
It does the way to Glory steer.

God's love the Fire, His truth the Steam
Which drives the Engine and the Train
All you who would to glory ride
Must come to Christ, in Him abide.

In First and Second and Third Class
Repentance, Faith and Holiness
You must the way to glory gain
Or you with Christ will not remain.

Come then poor sinners, now's the time
At any Station on the Line
If you'll repent and turn from sin,
The Train will stop and take you in."

G. m. Ain

JULIAN PETTIFER
Broadcaster

"In heaven there will be none of the following: biting insects or bad-tempered dogs, litter, cheap plonk, musak, bores, back-combed hair-dos, acne, man-made fibres, tight underwear, plastic flowers, plastic cups, plastic bags, plastic furniture, no plastic at all. There will be no junk mail or junk food but lots of junk shops to forage in. There will be no market research, no opinion polls, hair pieces, surgical appliances or PR men (or women). Neither will there be salespersons selling life insurance (of course not, silly!) or timeshare promotions. There will be no greenfly or cockroaches or talent competitions on the telly. There will be no Sunday papers with more than ten pages and no stupid Sunday trading laws. That will be heaven."

JOHN MAJOR, MP

Prime Minister

The P.M. couldn't stick it without any cricket . . .
"A day trip to heaven,
To see those gone before,
Where Grace can bat
And Hymn can bowl
As they did in days of yore

Hobbs would be there
With Sutcliffe at the wicket
Spofforth to bowl at pace
Ames to keep with grace
In a heavenly game of cricket

The sun would shine beyond a doubt
On a ground, tree-ringed and green
Felix, Fender, Hammond too
Cricket greats all on view
For my preferred celestial scene."

John Major

BELLA EMBERG
Comedienne

Bella's harmonious dream is...

"to meet up with my parents, my grandma (who had a great influence on my early life), my dear friends who unfortunately passed on before me. To meet Joan Crawford and the stars that have meant so much to me since first going to the cinema and theatre. Then going to a fantastic opera house to see a Verdi, Donizetti or Bellini opera with all the past greats singing. What a night that would be!! Callas, Melba, Flagstad, Caruso – with Toscanini conducting. Meeting Verdi. 'So beam me up Scottie' but only for the day. I love this world with all its so called faults and don't want to leave it just yet.

Who knows, maybe I will meet Jesus and God one day. Now that's a really interesting thought!"

LEONARD CHESHIRE, VC

Ex-RAF pilot and founder of the Cheshire Homes

"What no eye has seen and no ear has heard, what the mind of man cannot visualise; all that God has prepared for those who love Him."

1Cor. 2:9

APPARENTLY - IT'S THE ARTIST'S IMPRESSION OF HEAVEN BASED ON 1 CORINTHIANS 2, 9.....

MAEVE BINCHY
Novelist

The best-selling writer's fantasy is...
"to go into a place where everyone is good humoured and optimistic. People are glad to see each other – they are not critical or self-conscious.

I'd like them all to be full of chat – no polite silences or courteous restraint. I'd like God to introduce me to Hannibal and Napoleon – and that everywhere there would be a feeling that it all had been worthwhile."

KEN LIVINGSTONE, MP

The member for Brent East dreams of...
"no fear, no loathing, no Thatcher, no Tebbit."

MICHAEL BUERK

Television News presenter

Michael Buerk wants to relax...
"somewhere where I no longer get so many letters every day; many with worthwhile causes, but all making demands on my time so that I feel guilty about not having the space in my life to satisfy them."

THE RIGHT REV. MICHAEL NAZIR-ALI

General Secretary, Church Missionary Society

"When I arrived at the Pearly Gates, I was greeted with angelic music and a festal procession. Many there, including politicians, generals and artists were very envious. They took up the matter with the Recording Angel. 'When we arrived here there was no music or procession for us. Why have you laid on such a grand reception for this insignificant bishop?'

The Recording Angel replied, 'Fellow citizens of heaven, you must be tolerant and forbearing. Politicians, generals and artists come here all the time and come to stay, but a bishop comes but rarely and then only for a day!"

Remember it's not every day we see a bishop....

MENZIES CAMPBELL, QC, MP

The Scottish MP's angle on heaven is...
"a place where the salmon 'take' every hour, where the river is always at the right level, where the tackle never breaks, where the bull is always in another field, where the soup is always hot, where the water never gets into the waders, and where the net is always handy.**"**

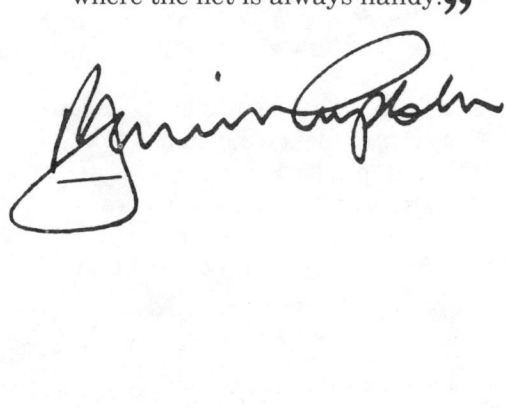

JOHN MORTIMER
Novelist and playwright

"My father always said he couldn't stand the idea of heaven as it sounded like some huge transcendental hotel with absolutely nothing to do in the evenings."

JILL DANDO

BBC News presenter

Jill is ready for...

"an early start. A 3am alarm call to avoid the rush and to make sure of a good seat on the rocket, facing the engine. On a long journey never sit with your back to the engine.

I'd be greeted at heaven's door by my mother and grandmother. I'm sure nanna would be coming to tea every Friday, just as before. There would be no telephone, no cars, no smoke, no fighting, no riches, no poverty; just peace, simple pleasures, sunshine, love and one guiding light. I expect I'd want to stay."

EDWINA CURRIE MP

The controversial MP wants to get away from it all with...

"a sunny day in Derbyshire; my family all at home, including my mother who is 78 and lives in Liverpool and doesn't travel much. A barbecue in the garden with friends – the fire being perfect, not smoky and not burning anything; a note from my secretary that the 250 constituency problems I dealt with last month have all turned out fine, that they are all going to vote for me at the next election, and that there is no post bag at all this week to worry about. I think that would be heaven. Thank God, we get close to it from time to time in this lovely area of South Derbyshire."

PREBENDARY MICHAEL SAWARD

Vicar of Ealing and Prebendary of St Paul's Cathedral

It's obviously a stunningly glorious place. Glistening and sparkling. Tree-lined river vistas down Main Street, the archetypal garden city, splendour and beauty shining out of every pore. Conservation orders on everything in sight. Peace, harmony, not a tear to be seen. Shouldn't be any problem promoting this place. It's a doddle!

Oh, oh! Just read the small print. It seems that the management is choosy. They reserve the right to refuse entry to liars, cowards, everyone who's into the occult and magic, all who misbehave sexually, all who betray other people's trust, anyone, in fact, who sets their heart on things rather than the City's boss. It's unbelievable! They intend to keep out anyone who is less than perfect.

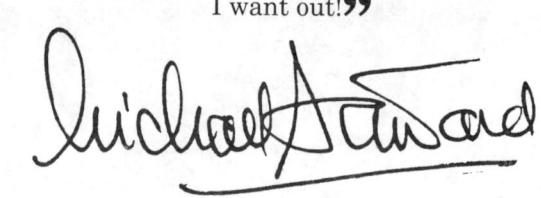

Good God, almost all my potential customers are for the chop. Heaven's going to be a hell of a place for people like me. Jesus Christ, what a set-up. I want out!"

RONNIE CORBETT
Comedian

“Selfishly I would hope that a day in heaven would be very much as a day I enjoy on earth: on a seaside link somewhere in Scotland, with the grass growing down to the sea, and the dunes and reeds and sea tossing and sky blue. I wouldn't like it to be like that all the time though, because if it did not rain at all the grass wouldn't remain green and the sand wouldn't stay soft under the feet.”

DENIS HEALEY, MP

For this poetic politician, heaven is...
"Thomas Traherne's description of this infancy when 'The corn was orient and unmortal wheat.' Harvested from his *Centuries of Meditations*. Another, perhaps less familiar to you, is Emily Dickinson's poem:
I went to heaven –
'Twas a small town,
Lit with a ruby
bathed with down
Stiller than the fields
At the full dew
Beautiful as pictures
No man drew.
People like the moth
Of Mechlin frames
Duties of gossamer,
and eider names.
Almost contented
I could be
'Mong such unique
Society

" I thought you were a little uncharitable to suggest in Brighton that I would be dead before the next General Election! "

Denis Healey
M.P

CAROLINE CHARLES
Dress designer

Caroline Charles's pattern for heaven is...
"feelings of light and warmth, with no clothes, because there are no bodies!

Limitless peace, goodwill and contentment with no divisions, because all is one."

Caroline Charles

PROFESSOR NIGEL REEVES

Professor of the University of Surrey European Management School

"Heaven, in all our minds, is usually the opposite of what we have and where we are. And for most people that means some state of complete indolence – resting on a cloud, sleeping in the sun, drifting, dreaming. But wouldn't that be boring! No challenge, no charge, just permanent inactivity. So my idea of heaven would not be that much different from now, but with an inexhaustible source of energy to teach, to read and to write, to travel and, I almost added, to enjoy life. But of course that's the point about heaven – it isn't life. So what we must do is to enjoy intensively those moments in life that are good, in work and play. That's heaven on earth and probably much more satisfying and memorable than heaven in heaven."

SIR CYRIL SMITH, MBE, MP

Rochdale's favourite politician has no weightier idea of heaven than...
"to be allowed to sit and snooze – no teeth in! Slippers on! No telephones – and to watch a soap opera to help me to sleep!"

DALEY THOMPSON

Olympic Gold Medallist

"I think I know what heaven is like – you see I've already been there twice. It is very near Shepherd's Bush; in fact it is Queen Charlotte's hospital to be exact, where I glimpsed heaven at the birth of our wonderful children."

WENDY CRAIG

Actress

Wendy Craig's vision is of ...
"a day spent in the company of Jesus. I have no other point of reference than walking this earth in close fellowship with the Lord, which makes every day on earth a trip to heaven. I read in the Bible about pearly gates, and a city of wonderful jewels, but I find all that difficult to imagine. However, a walk by a shining river, with the dew on the grass and my dog running ahead, knowing that God has promised never to leave me nor foresake me is more than enough 'Heaven' for me to be going on with."

DAVID ALLAN

BBC Radio 2 presenter

For David Allan, heaven would be...

"to swim out to sea off the Cornish coast and to discover that I was suddenly in a huge open air swimming pool. It is sunny and warm but not too hot and the pool is filled with happy folk of all ages enjoying themselves whilst many more are sitting on the expansive lawns surrounding the pool, including a host of familiar faces. I am especially delighted to find my mother and father in large deck chairs looking content and relaxed. There is no night and the fun goes on and on with brief breaks for refreshments and rest. On a small floating island in the middle of the pool is a genial old man dispensing drinks and snacks."

MATTHEW PARRIS

The Times columnist and parliamentary sketch writer

Matthew Parris's fattening heaven is . . .
"puddings: steaming jam rolls with lashings of custard – and hot baths."

GERALD WILLIAMS

Tennis commentator

Gerald Williams wants a front seat at the centre court of heaven in the hope of...
❝seeing a British man win the men's singles' championship at Wimbledon and knowing that the real thing will be overwhelmingly more glorious and infinite, because the Father has promised those who believe and obey.❞

SIR ALASTAIR BURNET

ITN News presenter

"I've no idea how big heaven is: most descriptions are wisely vague about that. As it's only for the day it won't matter.

The weather is a worry. I don't recall how it lay about me in my infancy so I'd prefer it to be mixed. King Arthur said it was where falls not hail or rain or any snow. But Jove, who used to claim to be the boss, is associated with thunder and I think it could be comforting. It'll be right if, in their glens on starry nights, the nightingales divinely sing and it's also all deep-meadowed, happy, fair with orchard lawns. Probably can't have everything.

I'll be reluctant to ask to see anyone in particular: Agamemnon difficult to interview; Mr Gladstone too voluble; and would Beethoven hear, far less understand, my German? Still, I'd like to see if Mary, Queen of Scots, was really six foot tall. And I'd like to come back (another away day to hell being arranged at senior citizen rate, too) with something comforting for the future. It's in Horace: blessed is he to whom the Gods have given just enough.

THE RIGHT REV. MICHAEL ADIE

Bishop of Guildford

A real Garden of Eden for the Bishop, for whom . . .

"Heaven will be a striking, colourful field of dahlias with no blackfly, no virus diseases, and no damaging winds. There will be just a riot of glorious and varied colours: the blooms will include the flamboyant giants, the spiky and angular cactus and the shapely decorative – all finding a place in a medley of glory. And there will be angelic gardeners who tend the plants with a care and a smile and point quietly to the Sun which ensures the warmth and the colour."

JEFFREY ARCHER
Author

No blockbusting thrills, just cricketing bliss...
"My day trip to heaven would consist of seeing Somerset play Yorkshire at Taunton, with Somerset requiring 24 points to win the Championship.

The match would end at 6.30 on the third day with Somerset winning in the last over and winning the County Championship for the first time in their history. Somerset would not only win, but Yorkshire would end up bottom of the table.

I suspect this would require the Archangel Gabriel to be umpire."

35

FRANCIS MATTHEWS

Actor

"Forgive me if my trip takes me to the predictable peace, joy, love and the fulfilment of every yearning of the heart and soul. When our breath is caught at the sight of the sunset; when tears of inexplicable joy well at the sound of glorious music; when love bursts in the heart at the touch of a child's hand – when these, or any incommunicable ecstasies take us by surprise, I believe we are being given just a glimpse of His face and of what He has in store for us.

I expect heaven to be like San Damiano, in Assisi; like a garden where weeds are wild flowers; like a feast of food and wine where there is no gluttony or drunkenness. Where I am with my family and friends and meet the ones I missed . . . St Francis, Beethoven, Noel Coward, Cary Grant, G. K. Chesterton, Philip Larkin (who will now know he had nothing to fear). But I think the friend I most want to see again (apart from my dearest ones) is Eric Morecambe who must have a special place in heaven for his joyous humour, because, as Chesterton said: 'There was something that was too great for God to show us when He walked upon our earth; and I have sometimes fancied that it was His mirth.' I expect heaven to be very unlike a solemn, lugubrious church service. I expect it, and Him, to be Fun!

How will I get there? With great difficulty! My 'heavenly influence for a day'? To ensure peace between all men, and the universal ability to get hold of a good plumber on Sunday."

Francis Matthews

AND JUST WHAT TIME EXACTLY DOES HE GET BACK FROM CHURCH....?

SIR BERNARD BRAINE, MP

Father of the House of Commons

> I am not sure that I want to make a day trip to heaven, especially as I have now arrived at an age when I must be quite near to finding out whether I have qualified for permanent entry or not. I suspect that a day trip would reveal that heaven is very much like the world we live in – in short it is what we make of it and what we deserve.

PAT SHARP

Capital Radio DJ

Pat's day trip would give him...
"a smooth journey and a quick visit, so I can avoid the rush hour, therefore getting home from HEAVEN without a HELL of a traffic jam!!!"

LES DENNIS
Entertainer

Les Dennis hopes for pie in the sky! He wants...

❝to arrive at the gates, and St Peter to say 'Ah yes, you're here for the tea party. This way please.' He would then escort me to a private booth in a most exclusive café where I would be reunited with my mum, dad and Dustin, my partner and close friend. The only tears would be of laughter as we remembered times we had spent together. I would tell them of the successes I had had since they had gone and they would say 'We know'. We would eat a glorious tea, all the things that are supposed to be fattening. Then before I left we would tell each other 'I love you' – something that is easier to say in heaven.

I would come to earth, not with a bump but with a clutch of lovely memories. As an added bonus, when I stood on the scales, I would not have put on a single ounce.❞

DOUGLAS REEMAN

Author
(also writes as Alexander Kent)

The popular novelist admits to feelings ...

❝of nervous anticipation. I have always thought of heaven as eternity, not a place of dates, times and routines, heavenly or otherwise. A place of sensations, of the ability to enjoy every level of beauty without actually being there as a physical onlooker. I write about ships and the sea, of the men and women who serve them. Can you imagine anything more boring than being pushed into close contact with millions of spirits of dead sailors, re-fighting lost wars from the Armada to Metapan? Millions and millions of them, a cross between 'This is (was) Your Life' and Disneyland. It should also be a place where you can, of your own choice, dip back into memories but without the pain and the sense of loss.

A day trip? I think not. I would rather drift.❞

THE MOST REV. DESMOND TUTU

Archbishop of Cape Town

❝I don't think we have too far to travel. In a sense we are already there. After all, this is God's world – I believe He is in charge and all that is missing is the formula, 'Thy will be done'.

If God's will was being done then there would be no difference between earth and heaven. But in spite of our disobedience God is here with us, it is still His world, He created it and a more beautiful and wonderful place as He created it is impossible to imagine. But we have spoiled this Garden of Eden and we long for a heaven of peace, joy and harmony beyond the pain and ugliness we experience and for which we alone are responsible.

Perhaps when we undertake our day trip we will be surprised and be given the chance to start all over again – with the right formula. What a heaven on earth that would be.**"**

THE MOST REV. DR ROBIN EAMES
Archbishop of Armagh

Heaven for the Archbishop would be...
❝the opportunity to find that there are other things in life than committees, correspondence and endless letters!❞

DR PATRICK MOORE, CBE, FRAS

Astronomer

The star-gazer takes a very down-to-earth view . . .

"This would be a journey to a place where the Church is not hypocritical enough to permit fox-hunting on its land. This, after all, is the nastiest form of cruelty, and toleration of it shows our Church on Earth to be utterly lacking in moral fibre.

So I hope to see it."

45

KRISS AKABUSSI

Sportsman

Athlete Kriss is used to winning races, but he dreams of losing the return ticket...

“Well to be honest, I am looking forward to a longer stay than just one day. I am looking forward to hearing these words: 'Well done, good and faithful servant; you were faithful over a few things, I will make you ruler over many things. Enter into the joy of the Lord.'

If I hear that, I know that I will have lost my return ticket back to the world.”

THANKS - BUT NO THANKS

RETURN TICKETS

KERRY SWAIN
Television Journalist

"In heaven you'd never have to make a conscious decision or a final choice. There'd be infinite possibilities – but no responsibility. In life one must either live in the city or the country, marry or not, pursue a career or care for children. You can't have it all. But in heaven you could be what or where you wanted in an instant – then change your mind tomorrow, or even in half an hour. Thus you could go from being a water skiing instructor on a Greek island to a sheep farmer in Cumbria to president of a multi-national company – just by wishing it. In the morning you could comb long blonde tresses, at night be a punk brunette! You could eat your way round Italy then lose two stone overnight! But you couldn't do anything for money, for power or to hurt others. There'd be no greed, violence or suffering. And finding yourself in heaven won't be a shock because it'll still look rather like the world we're used to."

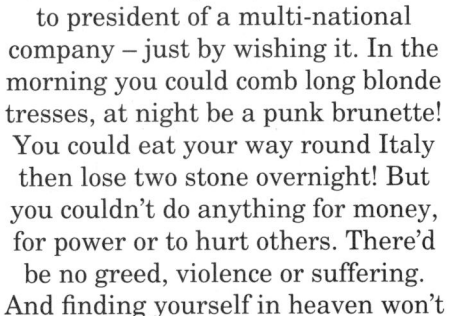

NICHOLAS WITCHELL

BBC Television News presenter

A peaceful heaven for Nicholas Witchell with...
"a not-too-arduous route via a Scottish highland mountain; starting just before dawn; complete with solitude, utter freedom, sensory stimulation, and no bagpipes!"

48

ANNE NIGHTINGALE
BBC Radio presenter

Anne dreams of double-decker delights . . .

"Bearing in mind I think you make your own heaven, or not, here on earth, I'd like it to be a huge bus-ride with all the far-flung people around the world whom I'd dearly long to see again. People, who for various reasons cannot escape their countries, Mahin Mostamand in Iran being the most important person to me. And to take all the political prisoners in the world on my day trip, on condition they didn't have to go back to prison. A bit idealistic, or what?"

THE VEN. JOHN WENT
Archdeacon of Surrey

"William Williams, an eighteenth century Welshman, wrote in a letter to his sister

'There is an ocean of happiness prepared for us and what we experience here is but a drop or a taste of that which we shall enjoy – a sight of His love is the cause of our love; and our thirst after Him is but the effect of His thirst after us; and our diligence in seeking of Him is the result of His seeking after us.'

It is my experience as a Christian not simply to know about the love of God at an intellectual level, but to experience His love at a deeply personal level, to be aware of being held, sustained, nurtured by the strong loving hands of a Father-God who has displayed the depth of His love for us in Jesus Christ. But the experience of God's love in this life, the experience of His peace, the occasional glimpses of His glory are nothing compared with the promise of entering into a full enjoyment of His love, His peace, His glory in heaven. Heaven for me is the promise of future glory!"

JILLY COOPER

Author

Jilly Cooper admitted to being so busy that heaven would be . . .

"a huge double bed and to be able to sleep for a hundred years.

The only other thing I would particularly like in heaven is for all the poor animals who have died through cruelty from humans or been put in agony by wicked vivisectionists, or been slaughtered in a horrible way, or just lost, could find a wonderful home there. If I had the opportunity I would like to spend most of my time in heaven going round and stroking all these animals and cheering them up, and seeing that they have a wonderful time."

JOHN SACHS
Television presenter

For John Sachs, heaven might be...

"a bit like avoiding relations at a wedding reception, except that in heaven there's hundreds of them, all queuing up to bend your ear about what you've been doing back on good old earth! So I'd probably slip off and go in the side entrance avoiding Peter and the management on the front door. They probably wouldn't let me in anyway because I had sneakers on or wasn't wearing wings or something! It must be a bit like Disney World – impossible to do in a day so I'd be selective about who and where I visited, you know, people like . . . Marilyn Monroe!"

WILL CARLING

Captain England rugby team

A touchdown in heaven for Will Carling will mean...
"an amazingly peaceful soporific atmosphere, with a subtle yet pleasing light. No traffic jams, crying babies, ringing phones and ever persistent pressmen! The transparent inhabitants float around on lead-free clouds, and definitely drive on the left! (All clouds have power-steering and air-conditioning.) Everyone wears crease-free white robes, but if you were extra-pleasant you are allowed a bright red sash, although you must not wear it after 6pm in built up areas. Wings can be hired at a rate of five good deeds and three smiles an hour, and you are presented with your wings once you have achieved significant humbleness (i.e. worn out your crease-free robe around the knees). Children always smile, never cry or run around, everyone gets out of each other's way when floating

down the pavement, and if you happen to bump a fellow 'transparent' everyone actually says 'I'm sorry'!!

Posters abound, depicting hell, with traffic wardens, crowded tubes, burnt ozone layers, a vacancy at Number 10 and a smiling Arthur Scargill! Pavarotti sings free of charge at every cloud junction, and Joan Collins actually looks 70!

Bliss!!"

THE RIGHT REV. TIMOTHY DUDLEY-SMITH

Bishop of Thetford

The bishop and hymn-writer hopes...
❝ to catch a glimpse of the vision given to the aged Apostle John, and recorded in the last book of the Bible (Revelation, chapters 21 and 22). Here is a hymn I wrote based on part of his description:

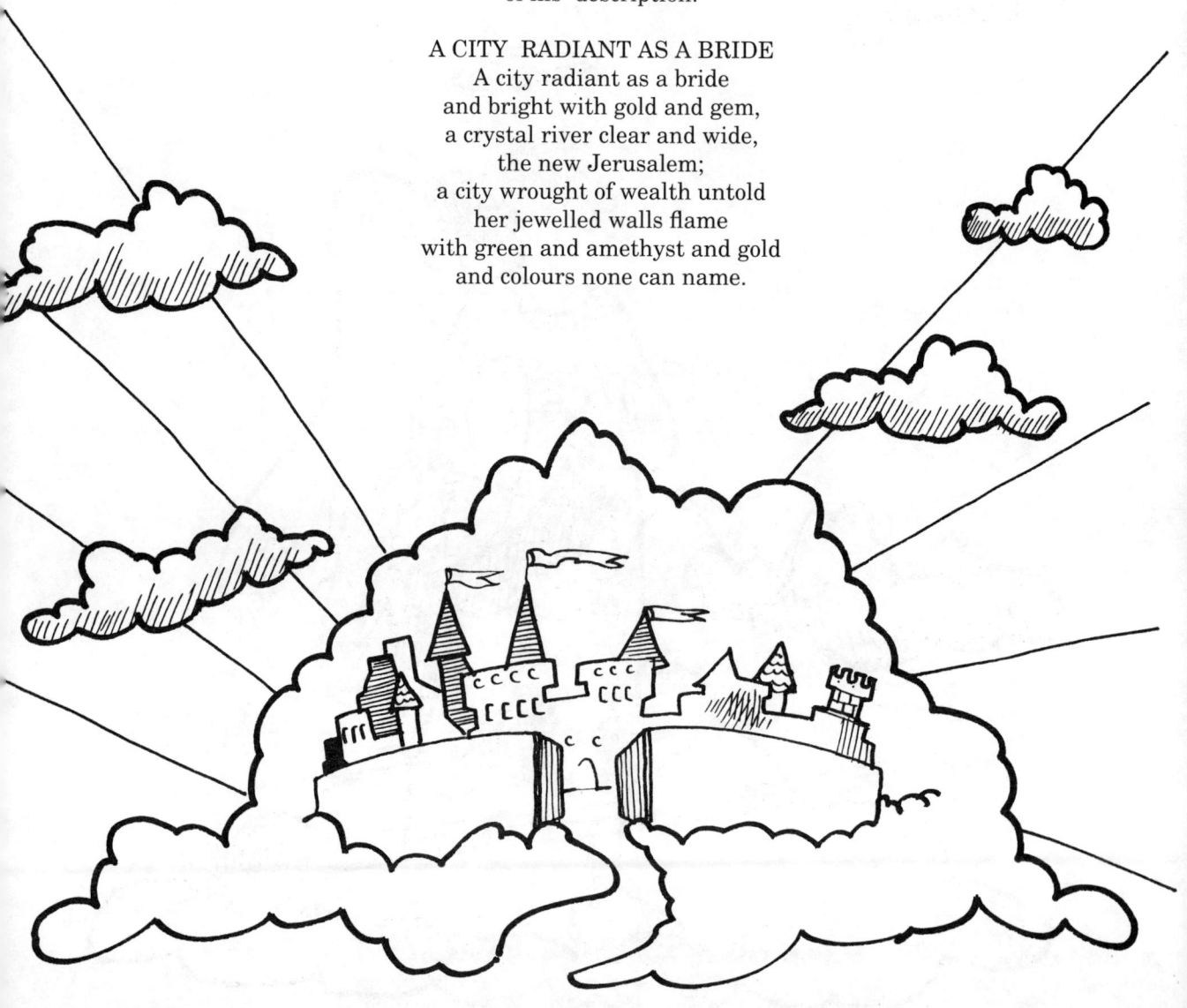

A CITY RADIANT AS A BRIDE
A city radiant as a bride
and bright with gold and gem,
a crystal river clear and wide,
the new Jerusalem;
a city wrought of wealth untold
her jewelled walls flame
with green and amethyst and gold
and colours none can name.

A holy city, clear as glass,
where saints in glory dwell.
Through gates of pearl her
people pass
to fields of asphodel.
In robes of splendour,
pure and white,
they walk the golden floor,
where God Himself shall be
their light
and night shall be no more.

A city ever new and fair,
the Lamb's eternal bride;
no suffering or grief is there
and every tear is dried.
There Christ prepares for us a place,
from sin and death restored,
and we shall stand before His face,
the ransomed of the Lord."

Timothy Dudley-Smith

STEVE RACE
Musician and broadcaster

It's a musical heaven for Steve Race, who hopes for . . .

"the opportunity to go to a rehearsal of the Heavenly Choir, and – who knows? – perhaps be offered the chance to conduct it while Saint Peter is otherwise engaged on gate duty. I might even be invited to choose what the choir should sing: namely an all-Mozart concert. (I might slip in a composition or two of my own. Or perhaps there isn't a Performing Right Society up there.) Whatever the repertoire, I can't think of anything more wonderful than the Heavenly Choir. Unless perhaps it's the Heavenly Symphony Orchestra. I've got some pieces they could play too . . ."

RUTH GLEDHILL

*Religious Affairs reporter
The Times*

Ruth Gledhill is clearly in heaven already. Her idea of perfection is . . . "writing about religious affairs for The Times."

SIR EDWARD BURGESS

President of the Royal British Legion

"It was my day for London. I was dreading it: the rush, the traffic, the thoughtlessness. But the sun shone and the air was crisp and clean. The day started to be different in the car park as I fumbled with 50p pieces for a £1 slot machine. A voice said, 'I can change those'. At the ticket office a normally dour figure said 'What a lovely day'. On the platform two young men in bomber jackets stood back for an old lady as the train came in. The train was crowded but a grey suited man helped the old lady with her case and gave her his seat.

So it went on; in London a car driver thanked a taxi for letting him into the traffic stream; an elegant woman complimented a station cleaner at Piccadilly on its cleanliness. The grin on the latter's face was pure heaven.

I felt my own relaxing into a smile. Then it came to me. People's thoughtfulness for others had made that dreaded London day a day trip to heaven."

MARGARET EWING, MP

The Scottish Nationalist leader just wants...
"to escape from telephones, faxes, journalists and piles of paperwork!

Since my own idea of hell is a world without books, I'd hope God would be kind enough to let me arrive with a couple of absorbing novels. To add to my relaxation I'd like to have a private stereo softly playing Earl Hines, Errol Garner and some Ray Charles.

I'd also like to transport with me the beautiful west beach from my home town of Lossiemouth, thus enabling a pleasant 'constitutional' walking along silver sands with all the sounds, sights and smells of a beautiful corner of this world.

I suppose, really, I want heaven to give me the chance to be slightly selfish and to do many of the things my busy life never normally allows me."

THE RIGHT REV. DAVID WILCOX

Bishop of Dorking

❝Well, it would have to be something like the best kind of 'day off' after I have been very busy. So – I want to be in the company of people whom I love very much. I hope there will be good walking country, mountains or moorland, and a characterful pub somewhere where I can have a pint and a ham sandwich. In the evening, I wouldn't mind sitting down, in congenial company, to listen to Mozart or watch a decent video over a supper which has been prepared for us.

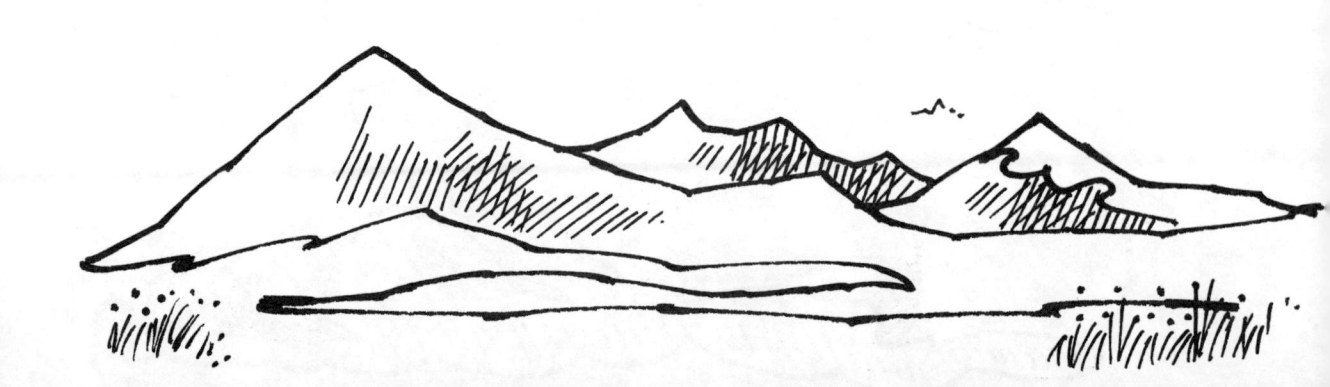

More seriously, what I am sure about is that we shall all get a lot of surprises – about who is there, I mean. And who is not!

The best description I know comes from St Augustine:

'We shall rest and we shall see
We shall see and we shall love
We shall love and we shall praise
In the End, which has no end.'

And the other thing I am quite sure about is this. Heavenly life begins here and now. So, with His help, let's get resting, seeing, loving and praising."

David P. Wilcox
Bishop of Dorking

BRUNO BROOKS
BBC Broadcaster

Bruno's space-age fantasy is . . .
"boarding an Apollo rocket and flying to the moon. Going for a space walk collecting fossils and returning with a splashdown three miles off Honolulu's beaches. Finish off with a party.

Could this be done in a day?"

SIR MONTY FINNISTON

Industrial business consultant

"The concept of heaven (and its counterpart hell) is beyond human ken – and mine.

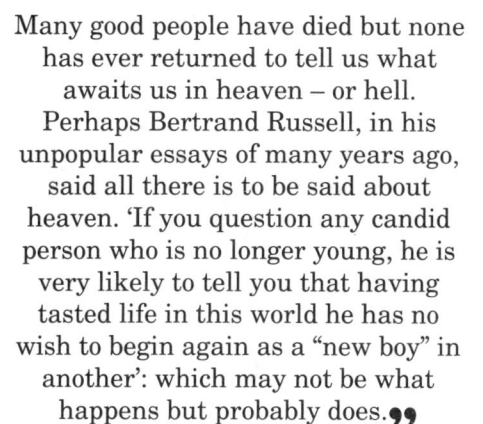

Many good people have died but none has ever returned to tell us what awaits us in heaven – or hell. Perhaps Bertrand Russell, in his unpopular essays of many years ago, said all there is to be said about heaven. 'If you question any candid person who is no longer young, he is very likely to tell you that having tasted life in this world he has no wish to begin again as a "new boy" in another': which may not be what happens but probably does."

Sir Monty Finniston died prior to the publication of this book. We trust that all his expectations have been exceeded.

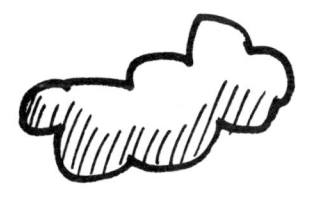

THE VEN. MICHAEL PERRY

Archdeacon of Durham

"A rich woman and her gardener both died. They were welcomed at the Pearly Gates by St Peter. He began to show them their heavenly mansions. They got to the gardener's first, and it was absolutely palatial. 'If that's what he's got,' said the woman, 'I can hardly wait to see mine!' So when St Peter showed her the miserable shack she was supposed to be occupying, she was highly indignant. 'How do you expect me to live in a hovel like that?', she asked. 'Sorry,' said St Peter, 'but that was all we could do with the material you sent up to us'.

If I could get a day trip to heaven, I'd like a little peep at the place I'm expected to occupy. Maybe it could do with improvement, and if so, I'd better see what I can do about it before I get there for good!"

SIMON MAYO

Breakfast Show and TV presenter

The Radio 1 DJ's heaven is . . .
"seeing Spurs win the championship, having the greatest curry ever cooked, and discussing the meaning of life with U2 over a few beers. In one day. Thanks."

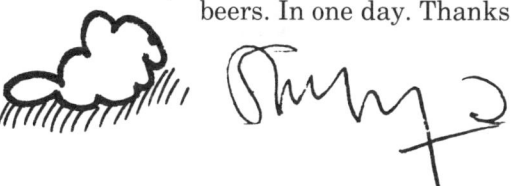

IAN PAISLEY, MP, MEP
Leader of Democratic Unionist Party

Belfast's famous and outspoken politician knows exactly what to expect:
"One of the greatest goals of man is to discover what heaven, the Throne where God sits, is really like.

Heaven is as follows:

Heaven.
There is a land where shadows never deepen,
And sunset glories fade not into night,
Where weary hearts shall win the boon of endless blessing,
And faith is lost in sight.

A land where sad farewells are never spoken,
Where every loss of life is richest gain,
Where stumbling feet at last shall find a haven,
And hearts have no more pain.

A land where those who sigh for long-
lost faces,
The loved of life whose going brought
us pain,
Shall find them in the brightness of
the Father's glory,
Where we shall meet again.

On that bright strand the blood-
washed ones of Jesus
Are safe; no more the weary feet shall
roam;
They find at last all that the heart has
longed for,
Within God's house at home.

The only way to arrive at this land where shadows never deepen is through the Lord Jesus Christ who provides us with a Route to His kingdom by accepting His invitation: that Whosoever calls upon the name of the Lord shall be saved and have everlasting life."

Jan R. K. Pewsley

YOU ARE CORDIALLY INVITED TO HEAVEN

Providing "THAT WHOSOEVER CALLS UPON THE NAME OF THE LORD SHALL BE SAVED AND HAVE EVERLASTING LIFE..."

R.S.V.P

THE COUNTESS MOUNTBATTEN OF BURMA

Magistrate

The Countess pictures an idyllic heaven. She hopes...
"to find myself in a beautiful, unspoilt, hilly countryside with plenty of trees and streams. It would be very quiet and peaceful with lots of beautiful birds and butterflies and flowers and fearless animals enjoying the warm sunshine as much as me.

But best of all I would be welcomed by my young son and my parents and all those I love who are already up there. In fact if I had a choice and those I love on earth were by then already up in heaven I would certainly not wish to use my return ticket from the day trip excursion!"

THE MOST REV. DR GEORGE NOAKES

Archbishop of Wales

"Heaven means many things to many people. There was the old lady who had worked hard all her life as a maid, who said 'I want to do nothing for ever and ever.' I would hope that heaven would not be a hive of inactivity! I have often wondered what Jesus meant when he said 'In my Father's House are many stopping places.' Does that mean that heaven is a continuation of the journey we take through life on earth? I would certainly expect it to be a place of excitement, joy, of life and movement. I would look forward to spending the afternoon with my loved ones who are there. There would be so much to say, but I guess they are already aware of what has happened since they left us. But the crown of the day will be to see Jesus as He is, in His splendour and glory.

After all that it will be sad to part again and return to earth with all its problems."

DAVID SHEPHERD, OBE, FRSA

Wildlife Artist

"First of all, the best way to get there (assuming that I have been chosen to go in that direction!) is to be hauled by my own 140 ton steam locomotive, 'Black Prince'!

When there, apart from enjoying meeting all the fascinating people who have, in many cases, been in residence for some time, I would also hope to meet the many wild animal species that man has exterminated. I could then talk to the world, if they would listen, about what man is doing to all his fellow creatures.

P.S. I trust that on arrival, I will not be mistaken for the Bishop of Liverpool as I often am!"

YOU'RE NOT GOING TO BELIEVE THIS

BERNARD WEATHERILL, MP

Speaker, House of Commons

❝This Punch cartoon of my distinguished predecessor's 'dream' in 1895 encapsulates my fervent wish to escape to heaven – just for one day!❞

Bernard Weatherill

PUNCH, OR THE LONDON CHARIVARI.—March 23, 1895.

a day trip to Heaven!
Bernard Weatherill
Speaker

RETIREMENT; OR, THE EASY CHAIR.

Mr. P. "WOULD YOU LIKE ME TO READ YOU LAST NIGHT'S DEBATE, SIR?"   Rt. Hon. Arthur Wellesley Peel (*drowsily*). "ORDER! ORDER!!"

["The original arrangement that Mr. Peel shall retire on the eve of the Easter holidays still holds good."—*Times*, March 16.]

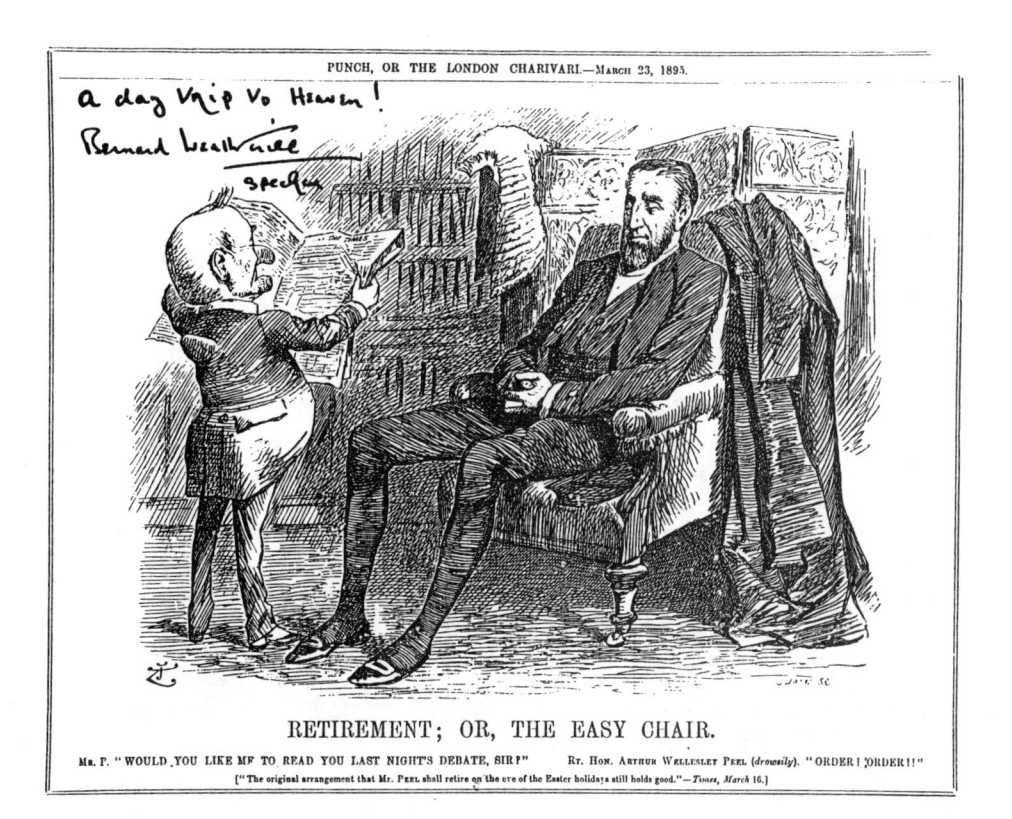

SUSAN HOWATCH
Author

Susan Howatch sees heaven as...
"sipping Dom Perignon champagne while the choir of Salisbury Cathedral sings 'Zadok the Priest', and willing an army of donors to contribute to the Salisbury Cathedral spire appeal fund."

MICHAEL NEALE

President, Institution of Mechanical Engineers

Michael Neale would like . . .
"to find a place where the skills of professional engineers are free to be focused on the creation of an ecologically balanced world in which all races can live a happy and fulfilled life. This will mean that heavenly laws will have overcome the economic ones, and made it possible for the skills that created the wealthy nations to be given to the poorer ones at a price which they can afford."

SARAH GREENE

Television presenter

The energetic children's TV favourite just longs...
"to be shown to a sunny beach with white sand. My sun-lounger and sun-shade would be already in place with lots of big fluffy towels. The sea would be warmish and clear blue. I would spend the day swimming with sea turtles and dolphins, having a delicious picnic on the beach and lying under my sun-shade reading my favourite books."

MATTHEW TAYLOR
MP

My idea of a day trip to heaven is . . .

DAME P.D. JAMES
Author

No mystery about P. D. James's idea of heaven. It's...
❝meeting my family and friends, having a long chat with Jane Austen, asking everyone how they managed to get in.❞

WELL — I NEVER EXPECTED YOU TO BE HERE

DESMOND LYNAM

Television sports commentator

Desmond's golfing paradise . . .
"would be if I was walking up the 18th fairway of St Andrew's, leading the Open Golf Championship by 8 strokes. Even I could take a 9 on the last!"

ROBIN HANBURY-TENISON, OBE

President of Survival International

"Heaven for me would be very like the tropical rainforest. The world's richest environment would in heaven reach its climax, amazing diversity would blend in perfect harmony and everything would have its full and integral place in the scheme of things. The people would live as part of all this abundance, respecting all other forms of life and living lives of ultimate affluence while owning nothing.

Such heavens do in fact still exist in a few places on earth and I have been fortunate enough to visit some of them. Sadly, however, the vast majority of the human race still fails to recognise heaven when it is all around them and instead of venerating it, they destroy it with chainsaws and bulldozers in the pursuit of Mammon."

DAVID ICKE

Sports presenter and Green Party spokesperson

David Icke's heavenly ambition is...
"to find the truth.**"**

PHILLIP SCHOFIELD
Children's TV presenter

"Two things would influence my trip to heaven, first a deep sense of curiosity. I'm always being told I use the word 'why?' more than any other, which sometimes drives friends and colleagues to distraction. If there's a 'why?' then I want to know it! One day in heaven would be terrific – to go on a fact-finding mission and come back – it would be amazing to be one of the few not to go 'one way'.

My second influence would be fascination and love of fantasy, whether it's films or books or imagination. I can't believe that heaven is a place in the clouds where everything is perfect and everyone wanders about sporting magnificent sets of feathery wings. I'm more attracted to the idea that it's a higher state of being, sort of – after all if nothing in nature is wasted how can 70 or 80 years of accumulated wisdom simply flicker out when someone dies? Basically I'm curious, but not ready for the full trip yet. Of course that's assuming I'm allowed in anyway!"

HAS HE GONE YET.....?
ALL THOSE QUESTIONS

COLIN BERRY

BBC Radio 2 broadcaster

Hopefully there are no hangovers in Heaven. Colin Berry's paradise would be...
"finding my greatest friend the late Ray Moore sitting on a cloud with a barrel of Burts Isle of Wight beer with a couple of blonde angels behind him playing 'The Best of Times' on their harps, and Ray saying 'I thought you'd never get here. We can drink the barrel dry – there's no last orders called here!'"

RABBI JULIA NEUBERGER

Rabbi and visiting fellow, the King's Fund

Rabbi Neuberger dreams of a heaven on earth...
"spending a day in this world without hearing or reading an expression of hatred from one international figure about another, or one religious or ethnic group about another. It would be a day of sublime, profound and analytical journalism without cheap jibes, and devoted to promoting alliances."

Julia Neuberger

AGREED — THAT PREVENTS HEARING OR SEEING DISCORD — BUT I THINK YOU'VE MISSED THE POINT

PHILIP HAYTON

BBC TV News presenter

Philip Hayton's day trip takes in . . .
❝Troutbeck, Inyanga, Eastern Highlands of Zimbabwe – a little bit of heaven on earth.❞

85

OUR FATHER, WHO ART IN TROUTBECK INYANGA EASTERN HIGHLANDS OF ZIMBABWE......

JOE GRUNDY

*JOE GRUNDY – tenant farmer
as dictated to EDWARD KELSEY*

Ambridge may seem like rural paradise to some, but Joe Grundy can improve on that . . .

❝My idea of a day trip to heaven is being given a preview of that Great Grange Farm in the Sky where all Good Grundies go: driven around on a spanking new red tractor held together with all its original parts and not a binder twine tied nowhere.

And I'd look to the South and I'd see acre upon acre of healthy orchard; every tree loaded down with God's little apples, all just ready to be turned into the most celestial cider.

And I'd look to the North and I'd see flock upon flock of sheep without a sign of scrapie nor fluke and the fleeces as white as the froth on a freshly pulled pint of Shires.

And I'd look to the East and I'd see turkeys beyond counting, plump and tender, without a mite in sight, and everyone of them bespoke – ordered and paid for by the Heavenly Host for its Christmas dinner.

And I'd look to the West and there would be rolling green pastures as far as the eye could see and the most beautiful herd of BSE-free cattle wandering in for milking.

And there would be other folk doing all the work and I wouldn't have to lift a finger.

Oh, and I almost forgot – the cowman's name would be ARCHER!"

THE MOST REV. DR GEORGE CAREY
Archbishop of Canterbury

The new man at Canterbury knows that heaven will mean...

"meeting Jesus: I love Mother Teresa's words. 'All the way to heaven is heaven because Jesus said: I am the Way, the Truth and the Life.'

But even bishops are sometimes reluctant to take day trips to heaven. Have you heard the one about the bishop who consulted his doctor: 'You must have a holiday at once on the Riviera', said the doctor.
'Out of the question,' declared the bishop, 'I'm too busy!'
'Well,' said the doctor, 'it's either the Riviera or heaven!'
'Dear, dear,' said the bishop, 'I didn't know it was that bad. It'll have to be the Riviera!'"

BOB CAROLGEES

Entertainer

Bob Carolgees confesses to a dream of heaven that is . . .
"totally selfish: I would gracefully glide in a hot air balloon over the most picturesque mountain range, accompanied by a can of everlasting draught Guinness, or maybe two, and land on the bank of a wide, clean, fast flowing river that contained thirty pound plus salmon, who thought my fly was the very nibble they had been missing all their lives. Having filled my bag and sported awhile I would climb to a cabin on a snow capped peak where my wife and children were waiting to sample my catch. Then we would all settle before the open fire with the finest cognac and talk trivia until sleep overpowered us all.

The problem with having run that through my mind is that several alternatives have occurred to me in as many minutes so that probably my idea of a day trip to heaven would be to slow the clocks down sufficiently so that a day lasted a week, or even a month – totally selfish."

STEVE CHALKE

Creator of the Christmas Cracker restaurants and evangelist

"Don't make me laugh. You've been done son! You'll never get past the gate. They don't do day returns, they never have done. How much did you say you'd paid for the ticket? They saw you coming – I bet they didn't offer to throw in a free car phone or satellite dish!

An Away Day Special. Take it from me, it's a fake mate. You can't get a return to heaven and back at all, so you'd best stop dreaming and forget about the whole idea now.

The only ticket that's valid for heaven is the standard one way single. Mind you, even then you've got to be careful, there are some very clever forgeries around these days. For instance, you can't half get stitched up by some of those American TV touts! That's the trouble with trying to pick something up at the last minute instead of planning ahead. You pay a fortune on the black market, think you've got yourself fixed up, but instead you end up out on the street, flat broke and in trouble with the law. As the old saying goes, "Play with fire . . . get your fingers burnt."

And you know what the really sickening thing is, don't you? After all that bother, as you're sitting in the gutter, you suddenly remember that one of your mates said he knew the bloke who gives the real things away to anyone who asks. Free of charge 'n' all. Makes you think don't it?"

STAN BOARDMAN

Comedian

"I suppose anyone who has been invited to heaven for a day would think first of meeting their loved ones who had passed away, then to have a look around to see what we have been praying for, if it lives up to its potential. I myself would probably want to see the boss and ask him what plans he has for me if and when I move in more permanently in the future. Probably my next question would be 'Do you play football here?' 'And any chance of a game' after he'd fixed my dicky foot. I'd want to play alongside Dixi Dean just to see how good he was with his head. Then in the evening, if they had one that is, take all my friends to a concert to see all my heroes, presented by: Arthur Askey, Ted Ray, and Jim Bowen (smile) finishing off with a couple of songs from Elvis. If we had a couple of hours to spare, pop into an Indian curry house and have a few lagers before catching the last cloud home."

BY THE WAY, HE DOESN'T LIKE TO BE CALLED "THE BOSS"....